100 Ways

TO ENJOY

Self-Care

FOR GENTLE
WELLBEING AND A
HEALTHY BODY IMAGE

FIONA FERRIS

Contents

FIONA FERRIS

Dear lovely reader,

As a female, life can be challenging at times. We are often responsible for a lot of different jobs. We put pressure on ourselves and perceive judgement from others, whether it is there or not. We take on burdens and responsibilities that sometimes are not even ours to carry. We may feel that we should look a certain way too.

We know our eating habits are sometimes not supporting our health and lifestyle goals, but it just feels good to eat what we want without overanalyzing things all the time. And then a pandemic comes along and throws everything up in the air. Even though things seem to have settled down we are still living with the consequences of that strange time.

Some of us have put on weight and getting dressed feels like a daily struggle. And then we think, *Well, why shouldn't I eat what I want? Are the food police waiting around the corner? I'm just going to do what makes me happy*. But still, we don't feel good when we eat foods that we know are not supporting our health, either physically or mentally.

I'm telling you; at times I feel like an experimental mouse in a box. Are you tired of all this rubbish too? Would you love to feel at peace with yourself on a daily basis? Do you feel like it's an obnoxious waste of energy to always be wishing you were smaller? Me too!

In this book I share with you one-hundred ways to feel good about yourself. To feel at ease in your skin and take exquisite care of yourself. To love yourself to bits and be happy no matter what. No matter how much you weigh. No matter which clothes fit. No matter if you're feeling fat that day. And to create a healthy lifestyle which will support you from this day forward.

We are taking it all back – the empowerment, the joy, the love for ourselves.

This is **what self-care is all about**.

Self-care sounds like a modern buzzword, but the concept has been around for a long time. Essentially it means that you prioritize your physical, mental, emotional and spiritual health and take care of yourself as well as you would take care of your children and loved ones.

Self-care is not selfish... but it can feel that way. Instead, think of your grandparent's generation. They didn't overwork themselves; they had time for leisure and rest, time to eat well, and time to socialize with others.

These days we are all so busy and think that we need to be productive every hour we're awake. I used to feel guilt when I did things purely for myself, and it coloured my enjoyment of activities such as having massage, painting my nails, or reading a book in the middle of the day. I'd think to myself, *Good gracious woman, just what kind of a Real Housewives lifestyle do you think you have? Go and do something useful!*

But now I see self-care as a necessity as well as a luxury. I feel grateful that I can have these moments of respite in my day, but I also know that they are available to many of us.

Most self-care practices don't cost anything, and they provide benefits for family, friends, and colleagues as well. Self-care can help us feel cosseted, looked after, and listened to. It can stop us from being so needy and *draw people to us* rather than push them away.

Self-care can be fun pampering such as booking a spa treatment or putting on a face mask at home, and it's also about loving yourself and *not being a meanie.* It's about cultivating a positive body image and doing things because they will improve your health and make you feel happier, not just because they might make you skinnier.

There are many benefits to getting into the habit of self-care, such as:

*Improving your immune system thus reducing
    illness*
Increasing your sense of wellbeing and positivity
Reducing stress and improving your mental health
Improving your confidence and self-esteem
Keeping you healthy throughout your life
*Being an example to family and friends when they
    see how well you treat yourself*

Imagine if everyone took the time to look out for their own mental and physical health and *we all felt good most of the time.* Wouldn't life be so much better if everybody did this?

What if, on any given day, you intentionally stepped back and thought, 'What do I feel like doing right now?' *and then did it.* Whether it was taking a rest, reading a few pages of a book, or going for a short walk outside to take in nature and some sunshine it would feel amazing, right? Like you are listening to yourself and not just riding rough-shod over your wishes.

Perhaps, like me, this is how you nurtured a ferocious sweet tooth that did your weight no favours. You were trying to find a spot of pleasure in your day because you had given yourself a long to-do list with no rewards. Enter... chocolate! Now chocolate is certainly welcome in its place, but for me it had become the primary way in which I gave myself something to enjoy.

But I found that when I focused more on self-care and what lifestyle habits made me feel good, my appetite naturally regulated itself. It went back to something that was enjoyable three times a day but then I forgot about it in between times. Snacking was lessened which meant I felt better physically, and my clothes fitted better. And more importantly, I felt better in myself.

For you, your pleasure time might be internet shopping or sipping wine. Like eating, these are both fine when they are done for the right reasons and in enjoyable moderation. But I know as well as you do that when you indulge in something too much, it doesn't feel good at all. Guilt and remorse are not fun emotions to surround yourself with.

So let's take loving care of ourselves starting right now. The beautiful thing about cultivating a self-care regime is that when we improve this area of our life, we find ourselves becoming brighter and happier, and a nicer person to be around. Those who are close to us benefit from our elevated spirit.

I do hope you gain loads of golden nuggets from this book and are inspired to lavish *your* precious self with love, attention, care, and kindness.

With all my best from beautiful Hawke's Bay, New Zealand,

Fiona

100 Ways to Enjoy Self-Care for Gentle Wellbeing and a Healthy Body Image

1. **Never go on a diet, ever.** A diet is not the answer, and a diet is not your friend. A diet is the ultimate in frenemies. Of course, many of us have been on a diet at one stage or another, and some of us are experts at *all the diets*. But if they worked, don't you think we'd be healthy, peaceful, and happy right now? Yes, I get that they can be useful for determining what an appropriate portion size is, but don't we already know what is helpful (fresh vegetables) and what is not (potato chips)? We already have a lot of information, and there is also common sense on our side. So let's all declare here and now, *no more diets for us*. We

don't need them. We can start by making healthy choices and small tweaks. We can swap a habit for something that is 1% healthier. Everything adds up, and it is sustainable too. Can I tell you, when I decided that I was never going to diet or be restrictive again, it felt like I'd been let out of *jail*. Hallelujah!

2. **Do what you love to do**. Gift your self pleasure in the form of happy satisfaction as you work away at something you enjoy doing. Make a list of all the things you love to do, reaching right back to childhood – compile everything you love into one big list in a pretty journal. Add to it as you remember things. My life-long list would include jumping on the trampoline, doing handcrafts, reading, wearing pretty perfume, having quiet time pottering at home, inviting a friend around, tidying my space to look neat and clean, and dressing fashionably and pretty. Come up with *your* list and do those things more often. (You will also find that when you keep adding to your list it could go on indefinitely!)

3. **Let yourself sink into a peaceful, feminine feeling**, and do whatever you are planning to do from that basis. You can be feminine on the outside, with dress, grooming, behaviour, and mannerisms, and also on the

inside, with a softness. You might be rushing around for no reason and don't need to be, so be there and appreciate the feeling of that moment. All it takes is a decision to be in your feminine, and from that, you will act differently and give off a different, more feminine energy which not only feels good, but magnetically draws people towards you as well. You will also find you get less burned out, because femininity is your natural state as a female. When you spend too much time in your masculine, it is taxing on your body and your spirit and you could feel burnt out. Be gentle on yourself.

4. **Choose fun physical movement**. Get in touch with your physical body in ways you enjoy. When we first bought our treadmill, I tried to go as fast, as long and as steep as possible. But I wanted to enjoy my treadmill time, not have it be a big ordeal and something that I dreaded. So I now walk in a relaxed and happy way for the length of time it takes to watch a television program – and I look forward to it each day. It's the same with doing a yoga class or workout on YouTube. Find a style that you like. For yoga I prefer the floaty, stretching yoga and gentle presenters over athletic, sporty yoga classes. And I love to find a workout where the vibe is glamorous, jazzy and upbeat. These seemingly frivolous details

make a huge difference. Find what makes something more enjoyable for you and discover what it feels like to look forward to exercise!

5. **Start moving S L O W E R**. Let yourself slow right down in everything you do – how you eat, how you talk, your thinking, your walking and physical movement speed, how you work – every single thing. I promise you won't be going at a snail's pace, but you *will* step out of that racing, hurried energy which can overwhelm your delicate nervous system. Even just letting yourself be still for a moment, softening your physical body, breathing out (we always hold our breath don't we!), dropping your shoulders and relaxing your muscles will feel *so good* to your feminine self. Do this as often as you need to as you make S L O W a part of your everyday landscape.

6. **Appreciate the beauty around you** and look at it with fresh eyes. Recently my husband and I went on a day-trip to a tourist town about ninety-minutes drive away. I was wittering away (as I do) but then stopped abruptly as I looked out the car window at the beauty of nature all around us. There were pine forests, snow-capped mountains beyond, a few hawks swooping, and it was just magical. In that moment I vowed to appreciate the beauty

around me no matter where I was. Of course, it's easier in the country, but everywhere has its own richness for us to notice and appreciate, if only we'd look for it!

7. **Choose water-rich foods**. Water-rich foods are primarily fruits and vegetables such as cucumber, tomatoes, celery, lettuce, apples, watermelon, kiwi fruit, oranges and peaches etc. When we eat them, not only are they lovely to taste, but they hydrate us naturally, and also cool us down on a hot day. One of my feminine lifestyle habits is to ensure I eat water-rich foods every day by making them look appealing to myself. This means buying small amounts fresh each week, storing them in the fridge, and washing and slicing ahead of time where appropriate. I eat fruit daily and include a serving of cooked vegetables or a side salad with my meals. Not only are these foods delicious and health-giving, but the high water content is great for your cells and your skin. It has been said that those who eat more water-rich foods look better – healthier and younger – than those who don't. Would you like to look more gorgeous just with a piece of fruit? Of course! Me too! Who wouldn't!

8. **Let yourself 'settle'** – just *be*. Sometimes we can forget that this is an option, a very valid option. There is no need to work out furiously

(or feel guilty because we haven't worked out at all). There is no need to be hyper focused on our goals. There is no need to be stressed about everything that needs to be done. We're just living, being and resting. We keep 'rest and play' as our mantra. You can still have a to-do list, and you can still be a focused, productive person, but coming at your daily life from a more relaxed perspective will help everything feel lighter. I've tried it for myself – often – and it works almost like a soothing miracle. And the more you intentionally choose to settle, the more habitual it will become.

9. **Change gears with music**. I like to play upbeat tempo music to get me going if I'm in the mood to do some tidying up or want to raise my energy, and when I want to relax it is delightful to shift gears by choosing a more relaxed sound to decompress by. While I am writing I play piano lounge music very, very softly in the background and it helps me be still and focus on my writing and my creativity. I also enjoy playing the same kind of music when I am reading. You can find my 'Dior Relaxing Music' under my profile 'Fiona Ferris' on Spotify, which I like to listen to while I am washing my face before I go to bed. I recreated a CD I was given when I worked for Parfums Christian Dior in the early 2000s. This CD was played while clients received a

facial from their Dior consultant. It is such beautifully relaxing music and I'm sure your feminine self will appreciate it as much as I do.

10. **Cultivate confidence *because*, not *in spite of*.** Imagine if you made a list of your biggest flaws, those things that you think mean you will never be truly lovable or attractive. And then, decide you are magnetic and adored *because* of these things. Your soft stomach? Your womanly hips? Your fleshy upper arms? What if you could decide that they are all desirable? And why shouldn't they be? I'm not saying to be silly about it and walk around pushing your stomach out like we used to do as children. But imagine deciding that your 'flaws' were no big deal, but are all part of Package You, which is a very exclusive and expensive product by the way. For me, I prefer to consider that I am curvaceous and sensual, rather than thinking, 'I could lose a few pounds'. Doing this changes your energy and how you come across, from apologetic to confident, both to yourself and those around you.

11. **Give yourself five minutes of stillness.** Lie on your back on the floor, and put your arms into a stop-sign position, also known as the cactus position. Basically if you were held up at gun point, how you would put your hands

up. Got it? Okay, now lift your arms off the floor minimally so you feel a slight, delicious stretch across the front of your shoulders. Stay this way for a few minutes and let yourself melt into the floor; actually let the floor support your body. Breathe easily and deeply. After a few minutes you can get up and carry on with what you were doing, but notice how refreshed you feel, how relaxed your shoulders are. Do this often, it only takes a minute!

12. **Read books that don't stress you**. Fiction reading is known to calm us down. I love to read a few pages of a novel before I fall asleep at night, and sometimes I even get quite sleepy if I'm reading on a Sunday afternoon, which leads to a short nap. But some books aren't relaxing. Some are far too gory and produce anxious thoughts. I tried a mystery crime series from a big name author once. What a mistake! They were so, so detailed in their gore that I still think about the awful details. From then on I decided to only read 'nice' books. A psychological thriller is as far as I go these days. One such book, a murder mystery that I really enjoyed lately was 'The Maid' by Nita Prose.

13. **Surround yourself with colours that make you happy**. What are your favourite colours? Why not fill your environment with

them as much as possible? When you need to buy something practical, see what colours they come in and choose the one that is prettiest. I needed some new sewing scissors and when I saw they came with gold sparkly handles amongst other options, I was smitten. My refillable water bottle is peony pink which differentiates it from my husband's lime green bottle. I have a selection of pretty boho blouses in cheery shades that I pair with stretch skinny jeans for my signature outfit. There are so many ways you can bring a little happy colour into your everyday life.

14. **Make makeup your art form**. No matter the level of makeup you like to wear (if you wear it at all), enjoy the process. Make it your little work of art every day. Look forward to putting it on and treat your time in the morning as a meditative art session, even if you have less than ten minutes budgeted for it. Every week or two wash your brushes with warm water and dishwashing liquid and keep your makeup palettes clean so that your products and tools are a pleasure to use. Try different colours from your palette not just always the same, and apply lipstick with a lip brush for that final flourish. *Be your own makeup artist.*

15. **Live the golden life**. I found unexpected feminine inspiration in old episodes of *The Golden Girls* recently. These ladies really are making the most of everything that life has to offer them, unlimited by being divorced or widowed or of being older in a culture that glorifies youth. They rest, relax and play. They sit outside reading a book or magazine, play cards together, sip a hot or cold drink, go out on dates, and enjoy their daily life. They are feminine and keep their looks up in an appealing way. They wear waisted dresses, shirt-dresses, palazzo pants, pastel colours, and paint their nails. They cheer each other up and have fun. They don't hold a grudge. They look for ways to enjoy their life and make it easy. They don't feel guilty for resting either. You may not be retirement age but there is no reason why you too can't claim a life that is easy and pleasurable. Why *not* live a golden girl life?

16. **Simplify your life**. You cannot live your best life when your home and your schedule is complicated and overly busy. Over the years I have worked on simplifying every area of my life and continue to do so. One example is a yoga studio I joined on a six-month pass. Even though I enjoyed the classes, I didn't like how much it regimented my week – it felt like I had a part-time job I had to get to each morning!

So I didn't renew my membership and instead found fitness activities I could do at home. Another example is indoor houseplants. I love them, and am always tempted by the glossy, healthy-looking plants at garden centres. But I can't keep them looking good. Plus they are just another thing that needs my attention. So I bought myself a couple of faux plants and I love the look they give to my home. (Don't worry, I still get fresh air from open windows and nature right outside.) There are so many little friction points you can address that will lend a sense of ease to your daily life. Find *your* sticky points, those areas which drain your battery, and work through them to find easy-care solutions.

17. **Cultivate a sunnier disposition**. Decide to put a positive spin on *everything* as you're doing it. Even if you already do, do it more so than usual. Talk things up, and tell yourself that X decision was the best decision ever. When you buy something say that you will receive ten-fold benefits from it (rather than have buyer's remorse). Perhaps you have areas where you have a blind spot towards your own negativity. I know I certainly do. But not anymore, we are sunning *everything* out. The more we do it, the better life gets. *Be the happiest person you know.*

18. **Soften *everything***. Soften your thoughts, your face, your muscles and your judgement towards yourself and others. Let yourself be softer every day. It will not only feel better, but people will be more receptive towards you. You won't feel the need to prove yourself as much. Soften your reaction times: instead of jumping to conclusions or being offended quickly, relax. Lean back. There is no need to be on high alert all the time. Let yourself be soft and help your nervous system relax. Doing this as a minute-by-minute practice when you need it will help you lessen stress and anxiety. *Let yourself be soft.*

19. **Live in a state of happy bliss**. I heard an excellent piece of advice a while back about not criticizing other people. As an example, imagine complaining to your husband about something one of his family members has done. Even if you are entirely justified, he will be torn between backing you up and protecting them. It's a natural reaction. By complaining about them, you are actually forcing him into sticking up for them. Instead, it would be far better to 'not notice' poor behaviour and even be 'surprised' when he points it out, saying, 'I didn't even see that' even if you totally did! I can see how not only would it be better for our relationship and have him want to protect *me*, but also that it just feels better to not focus on

other people's unpleasantness. It's something I wanted to do – be positive in my own life – but it felt like I was giving in if I didn't address any complaints. Isn't it wonderful that there is another way to handle things? We don't need to point out anyone else's faults. We can simply choose to live in our own happy state of bliss and everything will still be okay.

20. **Do your jobs as early in the day as possible**. One day I did all my household tasks at breakfast time – I prepped dinner and put everything in the fridge. I did a load of laundry. I made the bed, and even tidied the whole house. I did it all as quickly and efficiently as I could and *had the most wonderful day* as a result. Everything was done and I could enjoy my home and do other things. There was no end-of-day crunch time. Remember this when you are tempted to put things off until later, whether it's at work or home. It is not worth your peace of mind. *Do things early and enjoy the good feeling*.

21. **Lower your standards from time to time.** There is no rule that says you must do everything to the nth degree. *You don't have to do everything perfectly. You don't have to run yourself ragged sorting every little detail out.* It's just nice to let loose sometimes. Currently I am letting my rigid laundry standards relax a

little. Unless there is something really special in the wash, I've been putting all the colours in together. I 'folded' my sheets for next week's bed change by bundling them into a sort-of square shape. They'll still work! And today it's rainy so I am using the dryer. A dryer might be normal daily practice for you, but I grew up with a mother who used the washing line outside, and considered the dryer almost an unthinkable extravagance. You can only imagine the dryer up on a pedestal in my mind, only to be used under extreme circumstances and as a last resort. I feel so naughty using it! But it just feels good to play hooky with your standards sometimes. So, where can you 'let things slip' today?

22. **Cultivate your femininity**. We all have desires for ourselves, whether they are written down or not. For most of us we want to enjoy life, get things done, pay off debt, keep up with the bills and make progress over time. What I have found is that when I nurture my femininity, I reach these goals more easily. I nurture my feminine being by tending to my home, taking time for self-care and self-development study, and practising living in the moment. I feel happy and tranquil and am less likely to self-sabotage with snack foods or online shopping. Femininity is our natural

state as women, and when we ignore her she plays out. *Let your femininity be felt.*

23. **Feel tidy and clean**. I always feel more balanced when I have a tidy, clean outfit on, and my daily hair and makeup are done. I don't look like I'm going out to a special event, but I am presentable if someone calls by or I have to pop out. Having a clean home where everything is put away helps me feel more in balance too. There is not that sense of overwhelm which comes when you are always spying messy corners as you pass them. It takes barely any more time to straighten yourself or your home up, and the payoff is worth it. When you get into good habits it will feel like you have an invisible maid, tidying up wherever you go. *Be tidy and clean for a calm state of mind.*

24. **Sip slowly**. I love to relax with a glass of wine, but it doesn't feel good to go overboard. And these days at fifty-plus, overboard can be not much wine at all. So I'm enjoying a new regime inspired by my husband, who started alternating 0% beer with normal beer. I begin my evening with a tall glass of chilled sparkling water, and I sip this while I catch up with my husband about our day. When I have finished my water, I pour a small glass of wine. Because I have already quenched my thirst, I sip my

wine slowly and delicately. If I want another drink, I will have another sparkling water first, and so on. Often I will end up having only one glass of wine most evenings. It feels more ladylike, and it's definitely a worthwhile healthy lifestyle habit to cultivate. *Find a sipping regime that feels good to you.*

25. **Read vintage literature**. I have books on my shelf that I bought online from websites like *Thrift Books* or *Abe Books* or picked up in charity stores. Whether they are fiction or non-fiction, they are so delightful that taking a few minutes to read a chapter lifts my spirits and restores my equilibrium. Even just the age of the paper and covers of the books inspire me and are nice to have around, although you can buy a lot of classic books on Kindle too now which is handy. Amongst the books I have, my favourites are: 'The Woman You Want to Be' (1928) and 'How to Live Beyond Your Means' (1945), both by Margery Wilson, and 'The Magic Key to Charm' by Eileen Ascroft (this one was re-released as a new edition of a 1938 book in 2007). 'Orchids on Your Budget' (1937) by Marjorie Hillis is another delightful book too. And for fiction authors, I enjoy Grace Livingston Hill books. They are so chaste and sweet, romances from another time. One of her titles I read, 'Crimson Roses' was published in 1928. Nancy Mitford books are

smartly English, and Louisa May Alcott always soothing. *Calm and inspire yourself with vintage literature.*

26. **Design daily rituals**. Think about your lowest time of the day. Perhaps it is the busiest for you, or when your energy is most stretched. For me, it is late afternoon when my battery is the most depleted. Then, brainstorm all the ways you might be able to change this time of day from *stress* to *peace and relaxation*. Identify all the things you normally do at that time, and prune them as much as possible. What jobs can you move to another part of the day or be more efficient by only doing it every second day, for example. Can you delete or delegate tasks? Then work on filling in that time with fun, restorative activities. Sometimes we only do things at a certain time of day, just because we have always done them then. It's not until we step back and look at ourselves objectively that we can say, 'This is not really working for me.' Identify those areas for you, and *change your least favourite time to your favourite time*. Because you get to design your life to be exactly perfect for you.

27. **Create a feminine afternoon tea**. If late afternoon is your low time when you have the least energy and the most to do, imagine how wonderful it would be if this time was

transformed using the tip above. You could start by changing into clean, pretty loungewear, brushing your hair and tying it up off your face, and putting pearl or 'diamond' stud earrings on if you aren't already wearing any. You might freshen up your face with a tiny dusting of powder on your T-zone and some lip balm. You would spritz some fragrance on, lightly tidy the house, and put music on if it isn't already, then light a candle on the coffee table. You will already have done laundry, dishes, and meal prep earlier in the day. And, around 4pm you could make a cup of tea and read a paper book, either fiction, or glossy non-fiction. Choose something from your bookshelf to flip through, and have your journal and pen by you while you read, to capture any ideas and inspiration that come to mind. Doesn't this sound like a rejuvenating and pleasurable way to start your evening? You might not be able to do it every day, but that doesn't mean you can never do it. Work out for yourself how you can create a wonderful afternoon tea-time experience to look forward to.

28. **Be sunny in your mind**. Is it sunny where you are right now? It doesn't matter, because when you carry the sunshine in your own mind, you get to feel a warm glow on your face no matter what. You get to create your own

sparkle and shine from within. I love the power of positivity and of making my own happiness, because truly nothing feels better. Life feels easier, you move with more momentum, and even difficult times can be easier to bear. Regrettably we cannot avoid sad situations in life even with a sunny disposition, but I have seen first-hand that those with a positive outlook go further and seem more content overall. Choose to be sunny in *your* mind too.

29. **Elevate your vocabulary**. There's no need to become all prissy and proper or not be fully 'you', but we can all do a little better with what comes out of our mouths, and our shortcomings will be unique to each of us. When I think of this for myself, I could speak slower and more clearly. I could resist the urge to swear (curse) and use different words instead. I could annunciate better, and have a more pleasant tone to my voice also. What is it for you that you know could be nicer when it comes to how you speak and what you say? *Bestow yourself with the gift of elegant communication.*

30. **Let your life be easy**. Where was it written that we need to hustle every minute of the day and always look busy? I can't tell you the answer to that, but I can say that I feel it too. However, I have decided to train myself out of

it and I recommend you do as well. There is nothing to be gained in revving up our cortisol by feeling guilty if we rest, and always trying to put out the notion that we are a selfless person who puts everyone else first. Go on, I know you do it too! Instead, try this: with all the tasks you do in a day, ask yourself, *How can I make this easier?* Can you buy pre-made components of a meal? Not be so stringent on the housework? Delegate jobs to other members of the household? What if you decide to become a lady of leisure, even if only for an hour, and put your feet up? How would that feel? *Let go of the reins and let your life be easier.* Open the door to a more restful life just by asking the question!

31. **Change starts with you.** You have the ability to live a healthy, happy life. You don't need to feel trapped on a hamster wheel of being on a diet or eating out of control. There are many things we can't change about our body, but we can feel amazingly good when we change our beliefs and thoughts. Change starts inside our mind – there is no other way. We can't just change the outside; we'll rebound back to the way we were. It must be internal. When we cultivate self-respect and a positive attitude, and focus on our health and not a certain size, *miracles can occur.* I have felt it for myself and you can too.

32. **Curate a lady basket**. If you are anything like me, you like to have your favourite goodies with you. I had quite a few items that I carried from the living room, to my writing desk, to my bedside table. I was always balancing them or making two trips. And then my husband Paul said to me one day, 'You need a basket.' Such a simple solution! Within five minutes I found and repurposed a flat woven basket with handles and now have a luxurious lady basket to keep everything contained and handy. In it I have my phone, iPad and Kindle, a journal and pen, a notebook for book ideas, my reading glasses, and AirPods. You might like to include items such as tissues, hand cream, an embroidery project, and maybe a tin of mints or small chocolate bar. There is no end to how you can curate your lady basket. The rule I have for mine is that the items must be used daily, otherwise the basket ends up too full and that gets annoying. If this sounds like something you would find useful, I hope you enjoy putting together your lady basket too. *Why not curate your own container of goodness?*

33. **Find your style of feminine loungewear**. I love changing out of my day clothes before dinner; doing this helps me transition from 'daily doing' energy to a feeling of relaxation. I searched the phrase 'loungewear style' online

for new ideas, but found that most outfits looked like pyjamas! Personally I would rather resemble Elizabeth Taylor hosting a glamorous St Tropez soiree back in the day: imagine her in an elegant caftan or tunic ('resort wear' was a better search phrase I found, and there were plenty of inspiration images available as a result). Because it will be everyday wear it needs to be practical and inexpensive, especially since we have pets and I will be cooking in these outfits. I wanted to not be afraid to wear something fresh every single day. This is my fun project, to find – or sew – some silky, floaty pieces to feel like a luxurious and feminine goddess when I change at the end of the day.

34. **Nurture your inner child**. I'm more practical than 'woo-woo', but I love the concept of the inner child. Imagine her about five years old, the little you, and consider doing things that would make *her* happy such as reading a pretty book or working on a craft project. Give her boundaries and remind her that it's almost dinner time so it's okay if she's feeling hungry. Or maybe the little you needs a hug and a few words to reassure her that everything is going to be alright, and that you are here for her. Whenever you need to, nurture your inner child. She will be delighted

to hear from you, and you'll be amazed at how comforting it feels.

35. **Combine strength with softness**. Think about a ballet dancer. They are strong, yet graceful. They have put the work in to make their performance look effortless. *Be the ballet dancer in your own life.* Be strong on the inside and soft on the outside. You know what you will and will not put up with, and you have strong boundaries both for yourself and others. You show up in a gentle, gracious manner. You're not stomping around militantly telling people how you are, no, you are showing them by your actions. In my own life, if someone crosses an important boundary for me, I simply disappear. I don't need a big stand-up argument with them, I quietly withdraw myself. Many people are soft on the inside and brittle on the outside, but this combination can lead to burnout. Choose to be the opposite and keep that visual in mind. *Combine inner strength with outer softness for long-term resilience and peace.*

36. **Be an optimistic kind of lady**. Choose to be someone who looks on the bright side of life and who sees the best in people. Don't collect grudges and you won't collect wrinkles either. You know how you can see someone's inner world come out on their face as they get older?

I could see my scepticism and suspiciousness (which I thought was 'being realistic') was *not* going to age me well. I want my face to be soft and content as I get older, not hard and cynical. If nothing else, being a cheerful person just makes you feel happier, and life becomes easier. What's not to like about that? It takes practice to move from your old state, but I am proof that it can be done. I'm not perfect, but most of the time I am sunny and happy, and it's such a nice place to be. Be the optimistic lady in your own life!

37. **Work with your hands**. These days we spend a lot of time 'in our head'. We think at work, we are on the computer, and we scroll social media. There are also constant loops of thought as we remember everything we need to do. It's no wonder we can feel antsy and unfulfilled. The calming antidote to this is to create something physically. Chop vegetables for dinner. Tidy up. Bake. Knit. Paint. Weed the garden or plant plants. Complete a small decor project around the home. And of course you will have other activities that may suit you better. There are *so many* ways to engage in a meditative state and gain satisfying results. It feels wonderful to work with your hands and you will find that you feel calmer afterwards. Getting out of your head and into doing

something physical is very good for your mental wellbeing.

38. **Be in your body**. Similar to the tip above, choose to be in your body more than your head. Notice how you feel. Are there any aches or pains you are ignoring? Have you been sitting in one position for too long and could use a luxurious stretch? Stand up right now and have one. Or move your arms and do mini-stretches sitting at your desk. Relax your shoulders down and back. Drawing your attention to your physical body brings you into the present moment. Do this often and you will feel looser and more limber. Be 'in your body' as part of your everyday physical maintenance. Don't forget about her!

39. **Refrain from judging others**. The best thing you can do for your own body image and self-love in general, is to *stop judging other people*. Stop looking at how big or small they are, and whether they are better looking or worse looking than you. It can take some time to get out of this habit, after all you may have been doing it your whole adult life, and maybe even have inherited it from someone – did your mother do the same thing and remark on other people for example? Or perhaps on you? When you stop with the judgement, something magical will happen – you start to notice their

soul, their essence, their inner being. And, what will seem almost like a miracle: as you do this you will stop being so judgemental towards yourself too. Because what you judge others for, you judge yourself on even more harshly.

40. **Promise yourself you'll never again be tempted by the next new fad health trend**. Instead, listen to your intuition. Eat healthier to feel good if you want to. Choose fresh over packaged because you want to nourish your one precious body, your vehicle for this life, not because you want to be skinnier. Eat food with gusto, for it is here to be enjoyed. Put all the money you save on diet magazines, slimming clubs, and low-calorie food products into something that makes your heart happy – a pretty top in a style that suits your body type and colouring, a new lipstick, or some embroidery threads for a needlecraft project.

41. **Don't fall for the tricks of junk food manufacturers**. Their products have nothing to offer you except empty promises of good times. But don't ban them from your life either; there is a happy balance. When I remember how bad sugar makes me feel, I still eat too much of it sometimes and feel wretched. But when I buy myself a small treat

and enjoy it along with my normal healthy meals, I feel fine. Plus I have enjoyed a little luxury. It really does sound so simple and *normal* to do that, but for some of us we need a reminder every now and again. This is mine – maybe it is yours too?

42. **Live in your own feminine bubble**. My mum made fun of me growing up for living with my head in the clouds and making up my own fanciful way of being. Well now that I'm a grown-up and 'should' be more sensible, I've decided to take it to a whole new level. I live completely in my own fantasy wonderland. I rarely read or watch the news, I prefer fun, silly, happy movies and books, and I only want to be around 'nice' people, no drama please. And I do this while still being a kind person. There is no law that says we must take notice of all the upsetting things in the world. I care about others, of course I do, but if I cannot help them personally, I see no sense in needlessly upsetting myself. How I *can* help is to be a ray of sunshine to those around me, both in my real life, and with my writing. And I can only do this when I protect my energy. If you are hooked on the bad news and scary stories, perhaps revisit the media you are consuming. You may find you are more settled and tranquil when you refine your input. *Life*

*becomes more serene when you reside in your
own little feminine bubble.*

43. **Accept that your body is your body**.
Genetics play a huge role in how we look and
what our body is like. Of course we have
control over what we eat and drink, but there
is a set point that we will likely go back to, give
or take. From our parents and our ancestry we
get our height and many other factors
including our general size and shape. When
you think about it from a purely logical level, it
makes no sense that we would try to change
ourselves dramatically. Wouldn't we be better
to aim for 'healthy' and 'fit' instead and to
make the best of what we've got?

44. **Wear fabrics that feel luscious against
your skin**. Some of us are more sensitive to
how clothes feel, but I think we can all agree
that some fabrics feel nicer to us than others.
Materials such as floaty silks and satins, ultra-
soft cuddly fabrics, and even jeans can feel nice
when we choose soft, stretch denim that hugs
us. Sometimes I don't want to wear a certain
garment and have found the feel of the fabric
is the culprit. As well, make it a point to choose
fabrics that move pleasingly with you, for a
truly luxurious daily dressing experience.

45. **Ask yourself why smaller is better**. Have you ever thought about this? I have. Why is it that we think smaller is better and bigger is worse? Why are so many of us trying to lose weight, even a tiny amount, at all times? Why is it that the focus of our day is how 'good' we're being? Imagine the craziness of thinking shorter hair is better and we're always trying cut it when it grows, just to keep it from getting too long. It's as silly as always wanting to be a few pounds lighter. Consider why a normal body size, that sure, may have a few flabby bits, is really so bad? It's worth thinking about even if just to recognize the absurdity of it.

46. **Move your feminine body**. Certain movements open up your femininity and promote a feminine way of movement which suits our female hormones. The kinds of physical activity for this are yoga, stretching and Pilates moves. For those of us who charge around in our masculine by default (me), it can feel uncomfortable slowing down at first. But persevere, this kind of gentle exercise will balance you and help prevent burnout. And to go even further on the feminine side of things you could try belly dancing or hula hooping. I used to be able to hula hoop as a youngster but can't even keep the hoop up now. What is this saying to me! I am now on the lookout for

another and will be practising as soon as I find one to buy.

47. **Don't hide from food**, but don't overstock your home with all sorts of tempting treats either. Choose to stock your home with healthy foods, and make yourself work harder for the junky stuff by keeping it at the shop, not in your kitchen. Have it if you really want, but for the most part you will eat what you have around you. Be the kind of lady who keeps her home a well-ordered place of healthful items. You want the kinds of healthy foods which will nourish and enhance your physical being. Have a picture in your mind of a high-end whole food market – create an appealing mini version of that in your kitchen.

48. **Relax around food**. Food is neither good nor bad. It's just fuel for our body. Sure, some foods have been hijacked for profit, such as processed foods, and they will trick our brains into thinking they taste good. Some foods are better for us than others definitely, but *they're all still just food*. My encouragement is to relax when it comes to food and eating, and enjoy yourself when you do. Take the trigger away from food. The combined focus of relaxing around food, and the previous point of upgrading what you stock in your home will lead you to a more peaceful and happier path.

49. **Recognize how food makes you feel**.
Food isn't just a taste, it creates a reaction in our body. I can see this clearly when I eat sugar. It just feels so rotten! I don't eat it as regularly as I used to (which was daily), but I do still buy something every now and then, and, of course eat the whole packet at once. I can't not. I already know how I'll feel, but sometimes the craving for it overrules that. And I remember once again how yucky I feel afterwards, often for the rest of the day. How unkind is that to myself? Perhaps you can relate. So what's the answer? To think about your physical body's need, not what your mind wants. To consider *your body* first and put *her* experience as a priority. And, if you do have a blow-out, don't beat yourself up about it. Maybe it's exactly what you needed at the time. Give yourself a break from your thinking!

50. **Choose foods you know feel good**.
Scrambled eggs, a cup of tea, a big glass of water, a proper balanced meal with plenty of delicious fresh vegetables, a sliced apple with a few pieces of cheese. These are all foods I know feel well in my body after I have eaten them. This is the most basic human physiology test of all, don't you think? If an animal in the wild eats something that makes it feel sick, it won't be fooled by that thing again. It sticks with what it knows works well with its body.

We have lost that instinct, and it feels good to get back to basics – good wholesome food that nourishes and restores us.

51. **You cannot shrink yourself into happiness.** I know, I was disappointed too when I heard this, but now I know that it is *such a gift*. The gift of instant happiness and a feeling of peacefulness. You can feel joyful today when you see that dieting and wanting to be smaller is a trap forever more. Think about the first time you tried a diet; was it a long time ago? Did you reach your goal weight and are you still there today? For myself, no. Instead, dieting makes us obsessed with food. We eat more of it not less. Imagine letting all that fall away. How good does this sound? Let yourself surrender to that. Lean back, you are held. Life will support you. You can feel joyously happy today, exactly as you are.

52. **Be active.** I have found that the more I move my body around, the less I think about it, and the more I use it for what it was designed for: a very useful, functional tool in life. Sitting on my computer is fine when I'm writing my books, but not if I'm using it to pass the time aimlessly. Instead I'll get up and tidy the house, take the dogs for a walk, hang washing on the line, clean the kitchen, organize a messy area, go out to see people, do some gardening

and all the many things that fill a normal day. For you too, get up and do something, it feels so much better. You won't feel as stiff. And things get done too!

53. **Cultivate acceptance**. From now on, every time you look in the mirror, put clothes on, or think about yourself, work on accepting yourself as you are *right now*. Say out loud if you must, 'I accept you, I love you just as you are'. The opposite of acceptance is disapproval and rejection. When we refuse to accept ourselves until we are a certain size or our environment is perfectly decluttered and tidy, we are rejecting ourselves and disapproving of our very being. This resistance will *not* lead us to being slimmer or tidier. Try acceptance and approval instead and see how much nicer it feels.

54. **Don't talk about food so much**, even healthy food. Look forward to meals and plan them, enjoy them, yes, but then forget about them. Go grocery shopping, make good choices, go home and put your groceries away, then don't think about them again until you make a meal. Focus on other aspects of your life such as upcoming outings, friends and family you are going to see soon, goals and plans, your hobbies, and everything that is good and fun in your life. For some of us, food,

eating, and our body takes up a disproportionate part of our thinking, even if we don't realize it. Shrink that topic down and let other things flow into the space.

55. **Work on your goals loosely**. Goals are a very masculine concept, however I love setting and achieving goals – they're just such a fun thing to do – you get to dream up and design your life! How I have made them gentler though, is to work towards my goals 'loosely'. When I wanted to lose some weight, I did loose intermittent fasting, loose low-carb, loose everything. This means I didn't set a specific intermittent fasting time-frame, I just ate breakfast a bit later and tried to serve dinner a little earlier. Don't try to be too strict. Make tiny modifications slowly, letting change be permanent. *Make lifestyle changes to achieve your goals.*

56. **Keep on top of your life**. The more up-to-date you are with everyday admin, the better you will feel. In turn, this good feeling spills over into how you feel about *yourself*. You feel successful because your home life is largely under control. When I see something that needs to be done and think, 'I can't be bothered now, I'll do it later', that's the kind of day I feel lower. And conversely, like today, when I made the bed not long after I got up,

went for a walk instead of having a second cup of tea, and tidied a few things as soon as I saw them, I felt incredible. Like I could conquer the world! Resist the urge to 'do things later', bet on yourself instead and do them now.

57. **Don't assume that getting older** and gaining wisdom will help you have a better body image. It will still be there, and in fact can be exacerbated by the changes your body will go though as it ages. Right now is the best time to love yourself. Do what you need to do and you will have a much happier future, I promise. I know this because I am that person too. I never realized I had an unhealthy view of myself, I just thought I always needed to be slimmer. Then one day, I woke up and thought to myself, 'I would happily be the exact weight and look like I do right now if I could just find peace around food and eating.' And then that became my focus. Peace of mind, and health. It is *so* much more relaxing, and it got me to the same end goal of feeling happy with my body.

58. **Look through photos of yourself** when you were younger. Look at her sweet face. What a honey. Would you ever tell her that she needs to be different in order to be loved? That she isn't good enough the way she is? Thinking about this almost brings tears to my eyes,

because I'd *never* say that to her. Love yourself this much as well, today, exactly as you are. Keep a toddler photo of yourself somewhere handy and visit her often. Remember how much you love her. Love yourself. Treat yourself with *such tender care*. Know that you are perfect exactly as you are and you deserve to be loved, just because you're you.

59. **Make a list of self-care tasks** that you would love to incorporate into your daily, weekly or monthly schedule and then have fun choosing when to do them. You could have different categories such as your physique (workouts, going for a walk, stretching, healthy eating, spa treatments at home or out), your face (grooming your brows, following a simple skincare regime, exfoliating, trying new makeup looks, flossing), your hair (booking in for a salon appointment, upgrading your blow-dry technique), and your peace of mind (journaling, working towards your ideal sleep routine, reading fiction to relax, playing a musical instrument, doing self-development study). Doesn't it sound deliciously yummy to create *your* own self-care regime?

60. **Be a person who moves**. On the days that I've moved around more, whether it's going out, doing active tasks at home, or simply getting going on a project I've been thinking

about, I feel better about myself. And the flip side, on one of those days when I've barely moved at all – no walk outside, unproductive time on the computer, leaving tasks unfinished, I feel absolutely wretched. And the answer, I have discovered, is action. When I start to feel unmotivated and uninspired by anything in life, I get up off my butt and start moving. Movement creates a happier disposition, I truly believe that. *Our body wants to move.*

61. **Go with the flow**. Some days you will find it effortless to be perfectly healthy in your choices, and on other days you'll be hungrier, or eat less healthful foods. Some days your desk will be beautifully tidy and others, a complete bombsite! It's no big deal, that's how life is. I have come to understand that it's the *worrying* about how we eat and whether it's 'good' or not, or how tidy our house is that can do the most harm. Worry, anxiety and stress are not good for us, mentally or physically. We would do better to focus on lessening stress than obsessing over what we just ate or that we have three empty coffee cups on our desk. Do something fun, have a laugh, and know that nothing is permanent. Just because you were one way today, doesn't mean you can't be different tomorrow. *What a relief!*

62. **Keep a water bottle near you always**. I have always had a huge appetite for water and find it no effort to drink. However, if I don't have water near me I never drink as much. It's too easy *not* to go and get a glass of water. So I bought myself a pretty water bottle (a clear bottle with a peony pink lid) and it accompanies me almost everywhere. I keep it on my writing desk, by the bed overnight, and I take it with me in the car when I go out. I hand-wash it daily and refill it straight away. I believe that many sips is better than drinking huge quantities all at once, so having a water bottle to hand is the best option. Find yourself a bottle – you may already have one at home – and see how much easier it is to keep hydrated when water is always nearby.

63. **Start one tiny habit**. Something I have found so helpful is to choose one miniscule habit to implement, and only do that one change. It takes a mindset shift to get past the thought of, 'It's so small I may as well not bother'. But when you do, you will see changes happen effortlessly. One I wanted to start was weight training to tone up, but I don't like going to the gym and a proper workout makes me feel exhausted. So I decided to do a measly *five minutes* of arm weights every day using a small (1.5kg or just over three pounds) set of hand weights that I already had. Now I set the

timer for 5 minutes each day and do whatever movements I can think of. It's only five minutes so it's gone in a flash, but I can actually feel that it is doing something. And think about it, five minutes a day is 1,825 minutes, or more than *thirty hours* in a year. If you did this surely your arms wouldn't become *less* toned, and at the same time you are proving to yourself that you can create and keep a healthy routine going, thus improving your self-esteem. Win/win! Imagine starting a five-minute habit in one area of *your* life that you'd love to improve upon.

64. **Change one tiny habit**. Using the same principle as above, I improved a habit that I both love and don't love: my pre-dinner 'happy hour'. My favourite is to have a brandy and ginger ale along with a bowl of potato chips. If I could do this every day for the rest of my life I'd be a happy girl, but unfortunately it is not the most slimming nor healthy habit. Initially I bought only two bags of potato chips for the week instead of several. Since I only go to the supermarket once a week, I ran out after two days, but then I didn't mind having my brandy with no potato chips after that because I knew there were none in the house. Then, the next week I didn't buy any and now don't have potato chips at happy hour. The key was not to try to change the drink and the food at the

same time, I chose one and eased into it. Is there a habit that you can tweak rather than try to discard altogether? (Which we all know never works because no-one wants to feel deprived!) Try changing one small part of it and see how that works instead.

65. **Wear clothes that make you feel good**. Even if you're not at your ideal weight or in perfect shape, you will have at least one outfit that you feel amazing in. You love the colour of the pieces, they fit you well, you know you look good, and you feel comfortable in this outfit. Find all those items of clothing in your wardrobe and *wear them more*. On repeat if you have to. And the rest? Put them on probation. Become the kind of woman who feels great in her clothes, no matter that she might still want to improve on her health and fitness. What this looks like for me is a wardrobe of brightly-coloured pretty tops, and fitted stretch skinny jeans. I have half a dozen of each and they are all interchangeable. What is the outfit that you love best on yourself? Can you wear it more often? I was worried about wearing out my favourite red balloon-sleeve boho blouse but then I thought how silly that was. It lasts as long as it lasts, and in the meantime I get to feel like a million dollars in it.

66. **You get to choose**. Your ultimate self-care regime will be personal to you. You might love some of my ideas and be completely turned off by others. Dedicate a notebook to all your ideas and reminders and create your own bespoke self-care spa. Design a delicious range of treatments dedicated to lavishing yourself with pampering self-care, developing a helpful body-image, and cultivating your ideal healthy lifestyle. Take pleasure in fostering nourishing habits. Focus on making health-giving decisions most of the time. Be kind to your body. Treasure her. Love her. Pamper her. You are a Queen, a fine jewel. Take exquisite care of your physical self. Honour the temple you live in. Dress well every day. Adorn yourself for the fabulous life you live. Have fun putting on makeup and using up your lovely products. *Beguile yourself.* Be the sexy goddess you know you are at your core.

67. **Curate a supportive wardrobe**. If you have clothing in your closet that mocks you or reminds you that you used to be smaller, do something about it. If there are pieces you truly love and think that you have a chance of wearing again in the next twelve months, either hang them in a different wardrobe or store them in a suitcase or container. But if you own items that make you feel frumpy, or older than you are, donate them straight away. Buy

small amounts of clothing as you need things, and enjoy wearing them often. Don't save clothing for special occasions! Enjoy dressing well every day, no matter how you feel about your body. In fact, dressing well will *help* how you feel about yourself.

68. **Show yourself love.** Don't eat healthier because you want to lose weight, do so because you love your body and want to give her good sustenance. Don't go to bed earlier because you 'should' get eight hours sleep, tuck in with a book because you love yourself and want to feel coddled and peaceful. All the healthy habits you want to incorporate into your life but somehow never do, switch the thought to, 'I'm doing this because I want to show love for myself. I'm going to do ten minutes of stretching today because my body enjoys it and I love her'. Treat your body as if she were your daughter or little sister. Look after her, care for her, pamper her. She is so precious to you!

69. **Do what's right for you**. You aren't your husband or partner. You aren't your sister. You aren't your friend who might be naturally slim. You are you. Do what is right for you and don't feel bad about it. You *know* what is right for you. I always used to compare myself to how my husband would lose weight. He is very

masculine and linear in his approach, and I am not. So I would feel like a failure even though I was happy with how I was progressing. One day I decided to pretend I lived by myself and do things that worked for me in my own way. It made a huge difference to my happiness and success.

70.   **Create your dream lifestyle now**. Maybe you're a fan of journalling 'future self' inspiration like I am. It's so fun to think of a particular category such as your home, personal style, or health, for example. Then to list all the ways 'she' would be. Imagine if she had everything she'd ever wanted, what would *that* look like? And the best part, after you drink in the goodness that is your list of habits, ways of being, and any other details that would bring this dream lifestyle into reality, is to go through your list and see how you can bring any of these things into your life today, right now. Pick a few that are fun and easy and start them straight away. If your future self dresses in a way that makes her happy even though it might be a little over-the-top for others, dress that way now. If she goes out for lunch and enjoys a protein and leafy green 'goodness bowl' salad rather than a carb-heavy meal that makes her sleepy, eat that way now. It makes improvements seem so much more appealing. I did both of those things this past weekend

and not only received compliments on my outfit, but avoiding French Fries at lunchtime meant I didn't feel sleepy in the afternoon.

71. **Provide a feminine energy for your home**. Look at yourself from the outside in and consider your loved ones. I often think about when my husband gets home from work. I see him walking into a house that is serene and tidy, dinner is prepped, the person he loves (me!) is relaxed and reading a book, the atmosphere is peaceful and joyous, and there is soft music playing and candles flickering. Compare this to when I have mucked around and wasted my day, annoyed with myself at having let time get away on me and now I'm hurriedly prepping dinner. He has arrived home after a long day, changed, put his things away, gotten a cold drink for both of us and is sitting down wanting to relax. He offers to help with dinner because he says he can't relax until I'm sitting down too. It does not feel good! The silly thing is, I am also depriving *myself* of pleasure when I don't organize my time well. If this sounds like you too, just thinking, 'How can I provide a feminine energy for my home?' will deliver fresh vitality and have you effortlessly puttering around making things beautiful for yourself and your loved ones. *Create a feminine energy in how you are being in your home.*

72. **Keep returning to your ultimate desire**. If weight loss will lead you to your dream life, keep that goal in mind. Know that everything will be better, easier, and more enjoyable when you are a healthier weight. You might forget temporarily and let unhelpful habits sneak back in, but you can get right back to your fun plan. It doesn't matter how imperfect you are, and how many self-imposed bumps in the road there are. All that matters is that you *keep on going*. Refocus on your 'slim and glamorous' goal if that's what you desire. Pump yourself up again and again and you will get there.

73. **Let the habit of comparing yourself with others fall away** I had a moment one day and decided that regardless of how imperfect I was, I was not going to compare myself with others anymore. Incredibly, it felt like a heavy weight I didn't know was hanging over me just disappeared. I no longer needed to 'measure up' against others. I could just be me. Fabulous, flawed, imperfect me. From that point on I felt free to enjoy my life, even if I hadn't 'gotten there' yet. There is such freedom in deciding, 'Screw it, I'm not where I imagined I was going to be in this particular area (such as the mythical ideal weight for me), my house is a bit messy and I still talk too much, but I get to be happy and live my life. I'm not putting my happiness on hold

anymore'. When you do this, it's as if a bubble pops and you float away like Peter Pan, high over the rooftops. You can simply decide, 'I don't care. Others are themselves, and I'm me. I love me. I adore me. I'm going to live my best life and have the most fun. I get to do what I enjoy. I don't need to prove myself to anyone. It's all good.'

74. **Consult your future self for guidance**. Whenever I write in my journal as my future self, I am awed at how inspired, simple and effective her thoughts are. It turns out that I give really great advice! And you will find the same too, if you ask your future self what to do in a particular situation, or for an overall message. Last month I did this – asked for a general message – and here is what she told me. She encouraged me to enjoy my simple life, and that there is nothing else I need to 'do' other than live life the way I want to. She said to do what makes me happy such as reading a novel. She reminded me that having a clean, tidy environment always makes me feel light as air so to keep up with my admin, tidy up all those little loose ends, to organize my home, and clean and stage it – just for fun! She also told me, 'Feel blessed. You have a wonderful life. You are fully in charge of your own destiny and you deserve peace and happiness.' *Your* future self is a wise woman too, so see what she

has for you. I know you will love her message as well.

75. **Lose the habit of being all or nothing.** You don't have to be a one-hundred-per-cent clean eater or wallow in junk food. Amazingly, there is a mid-point between these two! To walk this middle ground, you can simply make the decision to 'be healthier', and lean into that. When I am in this frame of mind I naturally gravitate towards healthier options and have no interest in purchasing snack foods (which seems like a minor miracle when it happens). If I try to aim for completely guilt-free it feels restrictive, so mostly healthy with a touch of processed seems to be the middle way for me. For example, I love a smoothie, which consists of spinach, frozen berries and banana. I add raw nuts and seeds, and some olive oil too. But the scoop of Cookies and Cream protein powder gives it the 'yum factor' for me, plus the protein keeps me satiated until my next meal. It's the same with the raspberry flavoured sparkling water which I sip so I don't miss soft drink. And the packet cheese sauce I pour over my chicken and steamed veggies meal is another example. Look at your extremes if you have them, and have a think about what *your* middle way could be.

76. **Work on accepting people of all sizes and shapes**. Something that has helped me be happier with my own body, was that I stopped 'noticing' other people's shapes and sizes. Before, I used to take in that someone was bigger or smaller than me. I'd see how in shape, or not, they were. Then one day I decided to stop doing that. Just stop. Of course I could still be inspired if someone looked good and I loved their outfit, but the sting of them 'being in a shape I could never achieve' had evaporated. And it was only just a silly thought anyway. Now I don't even think about how others compare to me. I just enjoy my life, dress how I love to dress, eat how I do and get on with things. *It is so freeing.*

77. **Talk to yourself nicely**. No doubt you will have one or two (or fifty) negative comments about yourself rolling around in your mind. I certainly do. *I'm not thin enough. I should be healthier. I should exercise more. I should be more toned. I eat too much rubbish food. I should have a salad for lunch.* It's *so* tiresome having that awful, nagging person in the background telling me that *I am not good enough.* And I'm declaring here and now, no more. That voice is not real, they're just random thoughts floating past. Take them out of your head, write them down, and see how mean they are. Do you want to go through the

rest of your life feeling bad about yourself? Me neither. With the thoughts, change them to loving, supportive thoughts and read those to yourself instead. *I know you are capable. Let's go for a walk. Shall we make a delicious salad for lunch? I love you!* Be that supportive friend and talk yourself up. I promise you even though it sounds hokey, it works so well. You will feel better about yourself and that good feeling can only improve more the nicer you are to yourself.

78. **Let go of anger**. Something I have learned from listening to Rhonda Byrne's wonderful audiobooks (I have them all!) is to change negative thoughts to positive ones. Doing this helps dissolve feelings of anger, injustice, and unhappiness. I now say to myself all the time, 'Thank you for our quiet neighbourhood' or, 'Thank you for my peaceful life' and I focus on those thoughts, instead of the variety of daily matters we all have to deal with. I handle issues as they come up, whether it's a drama at a family dinner, or a leak that saturates the carpet, but I keep my thoughts light and elevated. I don't dwell on problems, and I rarely feel angry anymore. Let people be who they are, and focus on who you are. Focus on being a kind, thoughtful, grateful person. Definitely have boundaries, but apart from

that, focus on your own happy bubble and you will find anger easier to let go of.

79. **'Sorry, that doesn't work for me'**. Next time you are faced with a request you aren't happy with, consider saying so. You can say it in a nice way, or rephrase so that it feels more natural to you. And you can also ask for time to consider it: 'Can I think about that and get back to you? There are a few things I need to check on'. Just because someone asks you for a favour doesn't mean you need to say yes. Some people are just very good at stepping over the line, and you'll soon find that they are repeat offenders who also lean on other people. Distance yourself from them, and when necessary have a few phrases up your sleeve that you've decided on. Write them down in a notebook if necessary. I can't tell you how many times I've thought something and it was perfectly worded. But I didn't write it down and then it disappeared. So save useful responses when you think of them or come across them, and consider them an essential part of your serenity toolbox.

80. **Enjoy your daily life**. Let everyday life be *playful, relaxed, and in flow*. Identify when you are stomping around resentfully versus when you are happily getting things done from a peaceful energy. You will know the difference

between the two as you start to take notice of how you feel at any given time. Cultivate this intentionality and have it be an easy switch. By practicing it you will be able to live more of the time in a blissful feeling energy. Let life be more pleasurable in everything you do, even when it's only tasks and chores. *Let yourself enjoy daily life more.*

81. **Slow yourself down**. Most of us rush through our life. We've got an eye on the clock, a long to-do list, and a million things on our mind. I know I move too quickly every day. I always feel like I'm rushing, and I recognize that it's habitual and not even necessary most of the time. You too? Reminding yourself to slow down feels like the most luxurious thing ever. Slow down your breathing, your movements, and your mind. It takes only an awareness, nothing else. You will still get the same amount done, and in fact sometimes even more. *Slow down to be more productive.* Crazy, but true. Your nervous system will thank you too.

82. **Become someone who no longer gossips**. No matter the level of gossip you participate in, get rid of it all. Find all those little areas that fly under the radar. Treat gossip like weeds in the garden and eliminate them all, one at a time. It's hard at first, and if

you're like me, you will find there are so many seemingly innocuous areas. But keep on, and you will get them all. The way to know if you are about to talk in a way that is unhelpful is to ask yourself: 'If the person I want to speak about was standing next to me, would I say this?' If the answer is no, delete what you were about to say. Along the same lines, don't read gossip rags or follow gossip people online, just ignore it all. Go do something fun instead. And if you must get your fix every now and then? Spread good gossip. Talk others up when they are not around. Share positive news. Be that person who exudes radiance and happiness to others just by the way she is. You will have a different aura – more pure and joyful. It will feel good for you too.

83. **Let go of things that are out of your control.** How many times have you worried what others think about you? For me, it was a lot. I wanted people to think I'm a nice person and if someone didn't like me, it played on my mind. *Why not? What did I do to them?* Something that feels much better is to remind myself, yet again, that I cannot control what others say about me or if others accept me. They have free will. And so do I. Which means I will focus on what I *can* control: accepting myself and others, taking responsibility for my

actions, and finding my own joy and happiness in life.

84. **Appreciate what you have right now**. As much as I love to journal about the future me and also what my dream retirement lifestyle could look like in 15-20 years time, I also want to enjoy my daily life *now*. I sometimes forget that I have an incredible opportunity every single day to choose happiness and contentment. And I can quickly regain it by simply appreciating everything I have as I step through my day. I can appreciate that I now work from home instead of going to a boring office five days a week. I can appreciate that I love simple, inexpensive or free pastimes such as losing myself in a novel, or taking the time to prepare dinner while listening to a podcast. I can appreciate where I live and focus on the good points, such as being able to walk down the road and soak in nature. Even with my husband, I can make myself happier by only looking at the good things he does and not the things that might annoy me, because I'm not so perfect myself. *When you look at what's good, more good comes*.

85. **Stay in your bubble**. If you are a spongey, empathetic person like I am, it can be easy to feel fearful of war, natural disasters, inflation, rising crime, more people struggling, and the

general state of our world. But what if you just decided to simply 'stay in your bubble'? All any of us can do is live our life the best way we're able to and assist others by not falling apart ourselves. These world stresses can't last forever. Nothing ever does. The sun will come out again. And what use is constantly worrying about it? What good is that going to do for anybody including ourselves? Instead, find contentment in your daily routines and don't try to fix everything nor worry about the state of the world. It is what it is. Build for the future. Keep your frequency high and cultivate an air of light-heartedness. Focus on the good things rather than everything that could possibly go wrong. There is always good and bad, so why not focus on the good? There is *always* goodness around. It's just that sometimes you just have to search a little harder for it!

86. **Give yourself a reset**. Just as you would reset your bedroom by making your bed in the morning or your kitchen by tidying it up at the end of the day, why not *reset yourself*? All the things you were worrying about, all the tasks you haven't done yet, just *start with a clean slate* and decide *what is important in this moment*. Sometimes we drag so much behind us and it really weighs us down. Maybe that drag is in the form of a packed diary, a giant to-

do list, or by carrying things around mentally. Let it all go and re-decide what you want to carry forward. Let some things slide and they'll either come back or they won't. And what I have found amazing, is that some things I was trying to push myself to do, I magically regained enthusiasm for just by giving myself space. Give yourself the gift of a fresh start, right now.

87. **Slow down time**. Perhaps days go by without you even noticing, and hours pass like minutes. Or you hold your breath and don't breathe properly. If you often feel like you're running late, are behind, or disappointing someone... all of these things are reflecting your perception of time. Change how you experience time by repeating these phrases as needed: *Time flows freely and slowly. I feel blissfully relaxed. I move gently and at my own pace. I do one thing at a time. I breathe fully and deeply. I notice sensations in my body; what feels good, where there is discomfort. I look at the trees out the window and absorb their soothing green solid presence. Time is my friend. Time is good to me. Time looks after me. I have plenty of time. Time is abundant. Time is on my side.* I always feel more tranquil when I affirm words such as these. If you often feel like the day gets away on you, please, borrow my statements of being.

It's amazing how you can be the same person living the same life yet feel completely different: calm, peaceful, serene, yet still fully productive.

88. **Self-soothe without food**. If you are the type who deals with your emotions whether good or bad, by nibbling, you're not alone. It's such a common thing and I do it too. I am a person who has long had a habit to eat in order to feel better, even though I know it's not doing me any favours in the long run. If you can identify with this, what helps is to gather up all the ways in which you can calm your bored/busy/worried/upset (choose which is applicable!) mind in ways *other* than eating. Reading a book is helpful, but sometimes if you're sitting you might equate this with snacking, so getting up and doing something might be better. Relaxing your mind by going for a walk with an audiobook, or doing some stretches are ways in which you can quickly and easily come back to a feeling of grounded peacefulness. It's the grounding that is most important – we eat to ground ourselves, so find additional ways to do this other than by eating.

89. **Draw a line in the sand over past eating** and other unhelpful behaviours. What if the past never happened and we only remember it

in our mind. And what if tomorrow didn't exist either? What if all we had was this one day that we lived over and over. When we think this way it makes no sense to berate ourselves for things we did or did not do in the past, or compare ourselves from then to now. The past is gone and by thinking back to it every day we are dragging ourselves backwards. Wipe your mind clean and live from this day forward, every day. Give yourself a clean slate every morning and do the best with that day. Enjoy it. Be reborn daily.

90. **Turn a wretched day into a spa day**. We all have those days that feel like they're 'too much'. If you find yourself in one of those, cosset yourself with gentle self-care and declare your day over. Even if it's only the afternoon. Even if it's breakfast-time! I decided to do this today. I woke up wanting to do nothing other than write. My day hadn't started terribly, I just felt like a day off from my normal routine. A mental health day as they say. So I did. I gave myself a 'spa day' where my relaxation was writing. When you need a spa day too, as much as possible take anything non-essential off your list. Take your time doing the few necessary things. Enjoy your meals throughout the day, and dine in a peaceful manner as if you were at a spa. Sip herbal tea, read a book, and turn in early.

Perhaps rest is what you're really after when you feel like playing hooky from your life. *Give it to yourself with a spa day.*

91. **Consider that hobbies are a form of self-care**. Feeling good with your creativity and dreaming up future projects isn't just an enjoyable thing to do with your time. Hobbies are also a form of self-care, as much as having early nights or making healthy meals. When you find a hobby you love, you are enjoying yourself while you are doing it, but you are also clearing your mind. You get into flow as you do something, and your mind is settled. There is no room for worrying thoughts of future possibilities or past issues when you are focused on your task. Often we don't work on our hobbies because there are other 'more important' things to take care of. But what if we gave ourselves permission to take up a hobby again? Just for fun. What would you choose?

92. **Be in a tidy space**. This is a key factor in my mental health, and maybe for you too. For some of us, we notice every little thing, even if subconsciously. An out of sorts environment has *us* feeling out of sorts. That's why it feels so good when we straighten up. Even a five-minute tidying session feels fantastic. I tried it myself by setting an alarm for five minutes and

my kitchen and family room was completely transformed. If you too often ignore a messy area because you tell myself you don't have time and you'll get to it 'later', set the timer on your phone for five minutes and do it right now. Your kitchen counter, your work station, wherever you are.

93. **Choose flow state over hard work**. Think about this for a second: every job, chore or project you will ever do can be approached from either of these two angles. I am cleaning my house today, and writing a bit in between jobs while I have my mid-morning coffee. It came to me that at times in the past when I have resented vacuum cleaning and other household tasks, it is because I came to them from a place of dread. But this isn't the only way. When I chose to see my chores from a place of wanting to create a clean and lovely home, listening to a YouTube video on my wireless headphones while I worked, taking it at a measured pace and enjoying the satisfaction as rooms were straightened and small rearrangements made, flow state was entered. And let me tell you, it was so enjoyable. Incredibly, the work didn't seem as hard on my body either. Getting started is the trickiest part, but just begin with something and tell yourself you can stop after half an hour if you want to. But once you're doing it, as you

know, it's easy to keep on going, in that lovely flow state.

94. **Switch on your radiance**. Beauty is not just skin deep. Some of the most alluring women I know are not traditionally beautiful, but they have a quality you can't quite put your finger on – an inner warmth. They beam like sunshine even if they're just sitting there quietly. How I think they do this is that they reside in their body, rather than their head. They let their energy sink into their physical body. When I started practicing this myself, I felt relieved. Relieved to be able to rest instead of being in an overactive mind all the time. And yes, I felt the warmth for myself. Let yourself come down from your headspace and relax into your body. You have a whole five feet plus to live in, not just above your shoulders. It's called feminine energy and this is how you can switch on your radiance.

95. **Change your self-identification**. I have intentionally changed myself from someone who was cynical and sarcastic (I thought it was humour), and of course that all important 'realistic' (when in actual fact I was pessimistic). Now I choose to be positive, happy, lively, vibrant, light-as-air, sparkly and all those pretty things as much as possible. Because, why not? When you focus on the

bright side of life, everything becomes better. You will be happier. The people around you will be positively affected. I promise, give it a chance. Don't just say, 'Who wants to be a Pollyanna, that's fake'. It's only fake until you absorb it in. Negative thoughts are like weeds so you need to plant flowers (positive thoughts) to crowd out the weeds. That's exactly what a positive change does for your mindset. I'm sure if we could see inside our mind it would be a real thing. Mine would be a sea of cheery yellow daisies. What about yours? What do you see? And what would you rather see instead?

96. **Why not?** Whenever I start overthinking things, or my thoughts get on top of me, I notice this and try to let it all go. Who said we have to be responsible for every little thing in the world? Some of us take this burden on and feel guilt because we're 'one of the lucky ones'. Or we get down on ourselves because we don't eat perfectly, are grumpy with our loved ones, and sometimes do a less than stellar job with whatever we're doing. So, we're just human then. When I get like this, I nip it in the bud. I think, *Why the heck not, Fiona. Why not create my own dream world to live in? Why not make everyday life fun and creative? Why not decide to love myself no matter what? Why not make peace with my so-called flaws?*

Are you with me? Let's keep things light-hearted and enjoyable. Because, why not?

97. **Choose to be a goddess**. Imagine if you lived in a culture or time that glorified the female body which looked exactly as you do now. The exact weight you are, the colour of your skin, and how your hair looks. When we think of goddess it brings a vision of beauty to mind, but we can be that goddess from the inside. We can carry ourselves in a new way, and believe it or not, people will respond to us differently. One day I was practicing it without telling my husband, and he was noticeably different around me (in a good way). I was stunned! And all I had done was let myself sink into feminine energy and decide to receive pleasure from my day – and it was just a normal day. I did all my chores, but in a deliciously slow and joyful way. I truly felt as if I was being looked after even though it was me prepping dinner and feeding the pets. Remember the goddess that you are and let that be the place you reside in most often.

98. **Cleanse yourself of guilt**. Are you like me and feel guilty a lot of the time? Like you're going to get into big trouble or your life is going to fall apart when you are found out? That you are going to be *cancelled*? I always have this underlying feeling of guilt and it's been there

my whole life. It really weighs me down! For me I know it comes from perfectionism. Of remembering all the little things I did wrong in the past. I drag them along with me. But why? I have always been a kind person and never intentionally hurt anyone. But still, I think I could have done better. For those of us who are carrying a heavy backpack filled with guilt, shall we all take it off right now? Set it aside and open up the flap, only to find there is nothing in there. It was all in our mind. From today, we move forward with freedom and lightness. We are free from excess baggage. It's carry-on from now on, baby!

99. **Do what works for you**. I know that counting calories makes me crazy, and structured diets are my nemesis: they seem so appealing and promise amazing results. Then, after two weeks of 'structure' (aka prison), I lose my mind. Intermittent fasting can be the same for me. Sometimes I would say that diets have been responsible for me *putting on* weight, not losing it over the years! I know that simplicity, balance, and freedom work for me. If I feel like I need some gentle boundaries, I decide something like, 'I'm eating three good meals a day and not snacking this week', to jostle whatever little calorific habit I've fallen into. Eating healthy and living a healthy lifestyle looks different for everyone. Find out

what works (and remember what doesn't work) for you.

100. **Aim for total self-love**. Make this your highest goal: to be fully comfortable and happy with yourself *exactly as you are*. Without losing a single pound, without being better groomed, *just exactly as you are*. That doesn't mean you won't want to dress in a way that feels good, wear makeup if you enjoy makeup, and blow-dry your hair every once in a while. It simply means that you feel worthy of goodness just because you are a precious human being, not because of how good you've been or how you look that day. Self-love is caring for yourself as you would care for a loved one. Give yourself that unconditional love too. Just like loving someone else, you might get annoyed with them sometimes, but you will always love them, care for them, and want the best for them. Love yourself like that.

When it comes to self-care, different ways of looking after yourself will appeal on different days. You might need a good tidy up of your closet as a way of giving to yourself one day, and then the next you might require some floaty free time to simply dream and read. There are as many different kinds of self-care as there are people.

Please take the points from this book that resonate with you, and leave the ones that don't.

Build your own menu of self-care rituals that uplift you and keep you feeling buoyant. And change them up over time too – you won't always stay the same. From minute to minute and year to year, what you need will evolve.

This is how you can stay true to yourself, by listening for the clues and following the breadcrumbs. Your higher self has all the answers there for you, *just listen.*

50 Extra Deliciously Luscious Tips to Pamper and Coddle Yourself

And to finish, as well as thank you for reading this book, please enjoy fifty bonus ways to care for yourself on a daily basis. I always love to finish my books with a list, so I hope you gain a few more nuggets of inspiration as I send you on your way!

1. **Breathe deeply and well**. I have to remind myself to do this *all the time*. Lift your shoulders up and back and take a refreshingly deep breath in... and out. It feels so good.

2. **Book in some reading time**. Decide that on say, Sunday afternoon or Thursday evening you're going to read for an hour. On the sofa with your feet up. And then do it.

3. **Love how you live your life**. If others don't get you, that's okay. You don't have to change to suit them, even if they seem more 'normal' than you. The most important thing is that *you* love how you spend your days. (And normal is overrated anyway.)

4. **Inspire yourself to your goals**. Instead of strict plans, inspire yourself instead – with your own journal, from others in real life, via your favourite online mentors, from podcasts, eCourses and YouTube videos, and through movies and books.

5. **Delete toxic people from your life**. I did this for the first time a few years back very deliberately and *it set me free*. I still have to see this person in a group setting sometimes, but I have corralled them into a pen in my mind and they can no longer reach me mentally. It feels *amazing* and I feel safe from them now.

6. **Elevate your affirmations**. If you love the idea of affirmations but find them hard to believe for yourself, add 'I am learning how to' at the beginning of each one. So, 'I am living a healthy lifestyle' becomes 'I am learning how to live a healthy lifestyle'. It makes all the difference.

7. **Let yourself be light**. Sometimes you will feel heavy in your spirit for no reason. Let yourself illuminate with your glow and your brilliance. Float up. It's an internal change that you can do in an instant. Flick the switch!

8. **Adopt a rebel attitude** and say things to yourself like, 'I don't care if you think I'm not the right size', 'I don't care if you think I'm too loud' or whatever your insecurity is. Think it to yourself as a way of letting yourself know that you are okay exactly as you are.

9. **Try new styles and colours of clothing**; push yourself out of your comfort zone. I have noticed in photos that semi-fitted clothes are far more flattering on me than floaty styles which feel 'safer' to wear.

10. **Moods love to be fed**, so feed yours with the good stuff – positivity, gratefulness, and pure wonder at your beautiful life. If you accidentally feed your moods junk food – negativity, entitlement and sourness for example, quickly get back onto nutritious fare and feel better in an instant.

11. **Normalize what you want in your life**, such as fresh, healthy foods, a calming evening routine, and very little drama. Look at what you consider 'normal' now, and flip around what you

know is causing you long-term pain, such as a mid-morning chocolate habit. Normalize something different.

12. **Phrase 'discipline' in a way that suits you**. I have never liked the word *discipline*. It just sounds too authoritarian to me. So I chose the words self-respect and dignity, which have the same outcome but are softer and gentler.

13. **Never give up**. If you fall back into old unhealthy habits sometimes, cut yourself some slack, and get back to your healthy habits as soon as you can. Maybe you're going through a stressful time and you've used food or drink to calm yourself, but once you realize this you can let it go. Say to yourself, 'Thank you, and now it's time for something different.'

14. **Notice the thoughts in your head about how you look**. Some days they are brutal! They are not 'you' though, you are merely the observer. Let them float past and wave them goodbye if you don't like them. *They are not the truth*, they are only thoughts. Replace them with lovely thoughts; say nice things in their place.

15. Have you ever been teased about some aspect of your looks in the past, maybe as a child? If so, consider that your sensitivity may have come from someone else's own insecurities and can be

released by you with no harm whatsoever. **Hand back that judgement** in your mind and set yourself free.

16. **Choose the softest clothes you can**. You deserve the feeling of softness against your skin, whether it's underwear, a blouse, or your loungewear. Choosing the softest fabrics when you make a purchase is just one more way that you can comfort yourself every day.

17. **Wear colours that make you feel happy and light**. Notice when a particular shade looks pretty on others and see if it suits you too. You can hold up a top in a store – drape it under your face like the colour consultants do – to see what it does for your complexion. A failsafe method for me is whether I'm drawn to a certain shade – mostly it suits me when I am.

18. **Remember that wellbeing is your natural state**. Stop struggling with whatever problem is currently weighing you down and let wellbeing float you back to the surface.

19. Our female bodies go through incredible changes throughout our life, from childhood, puberty, childbirth for some of us, and menopause. **Embracing the changes as they occur** and having nourishing self-care routines are protective measures to ensure we

feel strengthened and positive when it comes to how we feel about our body.

20. **Create your own bubble of well-being** where you can feel light, optimistic, and hopeful. Lavish love on your family. Care for your home. Read happy books and watch fun movies. Do anything that makes you feel cheerful, positive, and confident.

21. **Let your mind become still**. Dirty water becomes clear by leaving it to sit still, not shaking it more. Find a pocket of calm in the corner of your mind and dwell there for a minute.

22. **Set up self-care stations**. On my writing desk I always have a bottle of water to sip, a tube of hand cream, and a small bottle of perfume. In a basket under our coffee table I have a nail file, lip balm, and hand cream. In my car I have a small tin of mints, a tube of hand cream and a lip balm. They are simple reminders to look after myself for a minute or two, and they bring me pleasure and comfort in return for a small amount of effort.

23. **Create a list of your favourite feel-good activities** and choose to indulge often. Pottering in my sewing room, reading a novel, painting my nails, putting on a face mask,

dressing up and going out for a window shop; these are some of mine.

24. **Set your life up for ease**. Imagine you are a process improvements specialist hired to go through a typical day seeing if you can make changes so that your life can run smoother. It's fun to do this from an outsider's perspective pretending it is someone else's routine that you are streamlining.

25. **Use up your lovely things**. We all have items we've been given that we just don't use. For me it's a new book I haven't cracked open, expensive candles, luxurious body products and gourmet treat foods. Enjoy them all. Don't save them for a rainy day!

26. **Inspire yourself to shine** when you've temporarily lost your mojo. Give yourself as many pep talks as you need. Forget about the past and focus on today, and your amazing future. It won't take long to get yourself back in the zone.

27. **Be your body's friend and supporter**, not her opponent. Love and enjoy the person inside your body too – she is amazing! Affirm that everything about her is perfect just the way she is. Accept yourself, *and* become healthier over time if that is your desire.

28. **What are you opting out of?** For me, I've decided I am opting out of a clutter-filled home, fear for the future, senseless guilt, diets and eating plans, how others think things should be done, and believing I should be a different weight. What weighs you down that you are going to opt out of?

29. Feeling negative about your body can lead to self-neglect sometimes. Of course, this will only create a further downwards spiral, so **start re-introducing small self-care practices each day** – full-body moisturization, keeping a bottle of chilled water nearby to sip from, and thinking loving thoughts about yourself.

30. **Declutter organically**. Instead of doing a big serious declutter, let your everyday decisions work their magic. Using items up when you have multiples, and not repurchasing until you get down to the last one is a simple way you can begin to lower the level of inventory in your home.

31. **Sparkle in your personal interactions** by asking questions of others, and promising yourself that you will only speak of positive anecdotes. Be that person who lifts others and yourself up by your manner. You can set the tone for any gathering by being calm, joyous,

and relaxed. Be the kind of person who puts others at ease.

32. **Start with Self-Care 101**. Self-care at its core is looking after yourself physically, mentally, and emotionally. Using these three categories as a starting point, come up with ten ideas that you'd love to incorporate into each area going forward.

33. **Lift yourself up**. Everyone has a bad day, but the key is to not let it turn into a bad week or a bad month. Take that day and make the most of it that you can, and know that tomorrow is a new beginning. Journal inspiration for yourself or read pages you've already written when you were in a better state of mind. How you feel is only ever temporary. Tomorrow will be a better day!

34. **Care for yourself as if you were a child**. You would nourish her with good food, ensure she gets enough sleep, dress her in a way that shows she is being well looked after, make sure she has playtime as well as doing her schoolwork, and take her outside for fresh air and a run around each day. We can do this for ourselves too.

35. **Create your own confidence**. Choose to walk with your head held high, and radiate pride

and confidence in yourself *as a person*, not a size. Let your inner beauty and individuality shine.

36. Remember that **your body is your home for this lifetime**. It is the shell to house your soul as you live this experience on earth. Putting it like that gives me distance from hyper-focusing on all the things that could be better about me. Instead I give thanks for the strong and healthy home I get to live in!

37. **Compliment other ladies** on something they are wearing such as a pretty top, earrings, or how they've done their eye makeup. When I do this with strangers (such as a bank teller or someone serving me in a store), they often ask me to repeat what I've said like they haven't heard me correctly; maybe because a compliment is so rare these days?

38. **Plan a day devoted to you**. Even if you never do it, write out in great detail how a deliciously decadent day *just for you* would look. Mine would have plenty of free time for reading, writing and sewing, meals would be catered, and I'd do a gentle, restorative yoga class in the afternoon.

39. **Accept the aging process as normal**, because it is. When you remember how

hormones and metabolism shifts over time you can then be realistic about how it is possible for you to look. Enjoy every stage of your life, even getting older. Many have not made it to your age and would love to still be alive. Rejoice in your beautifully imperfect self. Coco Chanel said 'The problem of aging is the problem of living. There is no simple solution,' which is so true, so why do we fight it and complain about it I wonder!

40. **Make your own sunshine**. Be that bright spark for yourself and others by working with what you have. Cultivate a cheery style with colourful outfits. Wear your prettier clothes every day. Inhabit the lighter side of life. Reframe a normal 'boring' day as a wonderful day to be alive.

41. **Shift your perception of self-worth** from your (external) appearance to your (internal) inner self. Study areas of self-development that interest you and have this be your focus instead of how 'young' or 'thin' you look. Enjoy keeping your body functional and healthy, and work on creating your glow *from the inside*.

42. **Listen in to how friends or family members talk about their appearance**. You may be unintentionally normalizing negative self-talk. When my mother says something unkind about herself, I say, 'Hey,

don't talk about my mother like that!' You don't have to join in with the complaint-fest, you can choose to be positive, or just say nothing.

43. **Many photos online and in publications are altered** to make them look more perfect. Even though we already know this, it's amazing how an image can make us feel less than. Remind yourself of this, and if you need to, turn off the screen and go and do something else instead.

44. **Reduce 'stimulation' in your environment**. For me, this means tidying my space, getting rid of clutter, and organizing things neatly. Even making my bed first thing in the morning makes a huge difference to how calm my mind feels. Creating a visually peaceful environment for ourselves means we will be able to focus more easily on what is important to us.

45. **Don't see healthy eating as boring**, or a punishment. Reframe it. See healthy eating as rewarding your body with beautiful food and clean, energizing water. Nourishing yourself with fresh produce. Gifting yourself nutrition and wellbeing.

46. Ask yourself this: *If I was to **dress in a way that made me feel good**, and no-one else had a say or could even see me, what would*

that look like? It's fun sometimes to give yourself a completely clean slate and *only please yourself*, no-one else.

47. **Book regular health checks**. Plan yourself a schedule for doctor's check-ups and blood work, eye health, dental appointments, and any body maintenance you would like to do. Don't 'think' about these appointments, just book them in. Be pro-active with your health and don't just wait for something to happen before you act.

48. **Absorb Vitamin D daily**. The sun has been made out to be a baddie, but I believe regular sun exposure in small doses is good for us. Because of this belief, I make sure to spend at least a few minutes soaking up the sun every day. Even in the winter it is possible.

49. **Tidy up loose ends**. This is one of my favourite self-care tips. I make a big list of things that are annoying me and complete as many as I can, as quickly as I can. It feels amazing! The kinds of things that make the biggest difference to me are sending emails, small clothing repairs, ironing, returning an item, making phone calls and other small tasks.

50. **Practice self-care every day**. Sustaining a good body image requires effort and persistence, just like anything valuable.

Surround yourself with body-positive people. Read books that lift you up. Feed yourself water-rich, life-giving foods. Dress to please your inner child with colours that make her happy. *Love yourself with all your heart!*

To Finish

For some of us, including me, we have spent much of our life wishing to be better, more perfect, skinnier, and prettier. Well guess what? That time will never come. All we have is today, and how we are today is how we are.

Why would we make ourselves miserable because we don't match an image in our mind that may not even be attainable for us? Why not decide to be happy anyway? Every day we spend hating ourselves, hating our bodies, is another day wasted. Another day of our life that we'll never get back. It's just not worth it. Instead, let's rejoice in today, and rejoice in our beautiful, imperfect bodies.

Will you join me in travelling into the future in a light and easy way? And in not letting the past weigh us down? Shall we all pamper, beautify, comfort, and look after ourselves with the most self-care ever known? Really spoil ourselves? Wouldn't that be a fun plan! To go totally over-the-top with self-care. Too much is never enough.

All that fresh food. Tons of fresh air and sunshine. Moving our body daily and keeping her limber and joyful. Snuggling up at night on clean sheets and snoozing happily for eight hours. Breathing fully and deeply because air is freely available 24/7. Imagine if everyone took self-care to the next level, the world would be an amazing place. And we can start with ourselves, because, why not?

Thank you *so much* for reading *100 Ways to Enjoy Self-Care for Gentle Wellbeing and a Healthy Body Image*. It has been my honour and my pleasure to welcome you here. I sincerely hope you gained inspiration from these pages, a sense of peace, and encouragement to love yourself more.

If you have a moment, I would be beyond grateful if you could leave me a review on Amazon. Even a few words are perfect – you don't have to write a lot. A review is the best compliment you can give to an author. It helps others like yourself find my books, and I'd love to get my message of living well through an inspired mindset to as many ladies as possible.

And if you have anything you'd like to say to me personally, please feel free to write:

fiona@howtobechic.com

Maybe you have a book idea for me, want to let me know what you thought of this book, or have even spotted an error. I hope not, but if you do find a typo, please let me know!

Think of me as your friend all the way over in New Zealand, cheering you on and wishing you well. You can be happier regardless of your weight, how you look or how old you are. You can feel 'perfect' exactly as you are right now, today. You have everything inside you to live the most wonderful life, and I hope you see that now.

With all my best to you, and I look forward to seeing you in my next book!

Fiona

About the Author

Fiona Ferris is passionate about the topic of living well, in particular that a simple and beautiful life can be achieved without spending a lot of money.

Her books are published in five languages currently: English, Spanish, Russian, Lithuanian and Vietnamese. She also runs an online home study program for aspiring non-fiction authors.

Fiona lives in the beautiful and sunny wine region of Hawke's Bay, New Zealand, with her husband, Paul, their rescue cat Nina, rescue dogs Daphne and Chloe, and their cousin Micky dog.

To learn more about Fiona, you can connect with her at:
howtobechic.com
fionaferris.com
facebook.com/fionaferrisauthor
twitter.com/fiona_ferris
instagram.com/fionaferrisnz
youtube.com/fionaferris

Fiona's other books are listed on the next page, and you can also find them at:
amazon.com/author/fionaferris

Other books by Fiona Ferris

Thirty Chic Days: *Practical inspiration for a beautiful life*

Thirty More Chic Days: *Creating an inspired mindset for a magical life*

Thirty Chic Days Vol. 3: *Nurturing a happy relationship, staying youthful, being your best self, and having a ton of fun at the same time*

Thirty Slim Days: *Create your slender and healthy life in a fun and enjoyable way*

Financially Chic: *Live a luxurious life on a budget, learn to love managing money, and grow your wealth*

How to be Chic in the Winter: *Living slim, happy and stylish during the cold season*

How to be Chic in the Summer: *Living well, keeping your cool and dressing stylishly when it's warm outside*

A Chic and Simple Christmas: *Celebrate the holiday season with ease and grace*

The Original 30 Chic Days Blog Series: *Be inspired by the online series that started it all*

30 Chic Days at Home: *Self-care tips for when you have to stay at home, or any other time when life is challenging*

The Chic Author: *Create your dream career and lifestyle, writing and self-publishing non-fiction books*

The Chic Closet*: Inspired ideas to develop your personal style, fall in love with your wardrobe, and bring back the joy in dressing yourself*

The Peaceful Life*: Slowing down, choosing happiness, nurturing your feminine self, and finding sanctuary in your home*

Loving Your Epic Small Life*: Thriving in your own style, being happy at home, and the art of exquisite self-care*

The Glam Life*: Uplevel everything in a fun way using glamour as your filter to the world*

100 Ways *to Live a Luxurious Life on a Budget*

100 Ways *to Declutter Your Home*

100 Ways *to Live a European Inspired Life*

Printed in Great Britain
by Amazon